AuDHD WOMEN

Navigating Life After Late Discovery

A Compassionate Guide to Living with Autism and ADHD

by Sarah Jones

DIAMOND DOOR PRESS

To all the AuDHD women
who spent years misunderstood.
You were never broken.
This is for you.

Contents

Introduction
The Name for What You've Always Felt

Maybe it started with a passing comment. Maybe it was a late-night article or a social media post that struck a nerve. Maybe someone close to you got diagnosed, and suddenly the pieces of your own life began to shift into place. Whether it came from a formal diagnosis or quiet self-recognition, something inside you finally clicked. And for the first time, your experience had a name.

Whatever brought you here, you are not alone.

More and more women are discovering the term **AuDHD**, and with it, a quiet kind of clarity. It's a word that describes something many of us have lived with for decades without knowing what to call it. AuDHD means that you live with both **autism** and **ADHD**. These are two separate neurodevelopmental conditions, but they often appear together. And when they do, they shape how you move through the world in ways that are easy to overlook, especially if you've spent a lifetime trying to blend in.

Autism affects how you process information, connect with others, and respond to your environment. It might mean you are sensitive to sound, light, or touch. It could show up as a need for routines, a dislike of small talk, or a tendency to go deep into specific interests. It might feel like social interaction takes more effort than it seems to take others. You may have spent years studying people, trying to understand how connection is supposed to work.

ADHD affects your attention, memory, energy, and sense of time. You may find yourself jumping between tasks, forgetting things you were just thinking about, or struggling to start something even when it matters to you. You may also have bursts of creativity, moments of hyperfocus, or days when everything clicks. But those moments might be hard to predict or repeat.

When you live with both autism and ADHD, life can feel confusing in ways that are hard to explain. You may crave structure but struggle to keep it. You might be deeply sensitive, but also restless. You may need quiet but find your mind never slows down. You might have spent years thinking you were just anxious, or disorganized, or too intense. Maybe you were called gifted. Maybe you were called lazy. Maybe you've heard both, sometimes in the same day.

Many women who are AuDHD go undiagnosed until adulthood. Not because the signs weren't there, but because they didn't match what most people were taught to look for. Girls are often expected to be quiet, polite, and adaptable. If you learned how to meet those expectations, even at a high personal cost, it's possible no one ever asked what it was costing you.

It's also important to acknowledge that the path to understanding AuDHD can be even more complex for women who navigate multiple identities. Women of color, LGBTQ+ women, women from working-class backgrounds, and those facing other forms of marginalization often encounter additional barriers to recognition and diagnosis. Cultural expectations, economic access to healthcare, and biases within medical systems can further delay or complicate the journey to understanding. While this book focuses primarily on the shared experiences of AuDHD women, it's written with deep respect for the reality that neurodivergence intersects with many other aspects of identity, and that some women face compounded challenges in being seen and understood.

In many ways, being AuDHD can come with powerful gifts. Many late-diagnosed women discover that their deep empathy, creative problem-solving, strong pattern recognition, and intense curiosity have always been part of how their brain works. These traits may have gone unnoticed or undervalued in environments that rewarded conformity, but they are strengths that can lead to meaningful relationships, original ideas, and intuitive insight. Recognizing these qualities isn't about ignoring the challenges, it's about making room for a fuller, more accurate picture of who you are.

When the truth finally comes into focus, the emotional impact can be surprisingly strong. There's often a wave of relief. Finally, something explains the invisible effort it took to get through each day. But there can also be grief for the time lost, and for the girl or woman you were trying so hard to be. There may be anger at the missed signs, or at the systems that let you down. And eventually, there is clarity. Things begin to make sense, not just in the present, but looking back across your entire life.

You are not behind. You were never broken. You were simply misunderstood.

This book is a starting place, not a rulebook. It's not medical advice and it's not a clinical textbook. Any guidance about your health or care should come from a qualified professional. What you'll find here is meant to gently guide, not diagnose. It's for women who have worked hard to be "okay" without always being understood, and who want language and insight that feels like it fits. It's not a list of what's wrong. It's an invitation to see yourself with more care and less judgment, and to slowly build a life that works for the way your brain and body truly are.

You'll notice journal prompts scattered throughout

these pages. Think of them as gentle invitations rather than homework. Use them when they feel helpful, skip them when they don't.

*

Journal Prompt

What changed when I first heard the term AuDHD?

Chapter 1
The Overlap of Autism and ADHD

When people first learn about autism or ADHD, they're often introduced to them as two separate conditions. They might imagine a child with autism who doesn't speak, or a boy with ADHD who can't sit still in class. These narrow ideas are based on outdated stereotypes, and they leave out a wide range of real-life experiences. Especially the experiences of adult women.

What many people don't realize is that **autism and ADHD frequently show up together**. In fact, some research suggests that as many as half of those diagnosed with autism also meet the criteria for ADHD. But when both are present in the same person, it can be harder to recognize. The traits overlap, and sometimes they even seem to contradict each other. That's part of what makes **AuDHD** so hard to see from the outside.

And often hard to name from the inside, too.

How the Traits Blend

Living with AuDHD means you are navigating a combination of neurological traits that influence how you process the world. You might have a strong need for routine and predictability, while also struggling to stay organized. You might feel deeply tuned in to subtle sensory information, but constantly distracted by it. You might get completely absorbed in something you love, then feel unable to return to it the next day.

Let's look more closely at some of the traits that often show up in AuDHD women:

Sensory Sensitivity

You may find certain sounds unbearable, or get overwhelmed in crowded stores or bright rooms. You might avoid certain fabrics, food textures, or even conversations that feel too loud or too fast. *Sensory sensitivity* doesn't just come in, it comes in strong and fast. This can lead to shutdowns or meltdowns that are hard to explain, especially when others think you're "overreacting."

Emotional Intensity

Many AuDHD women feel things with deep *emotional*

intensity. You might be moved to tears by music or crushed by a comment that others forget in five minutes. Your inner emotional world may be rich, fast-moving, and hard to regulate. You might experience emotional whiplash: intense joy followed by sudden overwhelm. Sometimes these shifts are tied to sensory triggers or social confusion, and they often go unseen.

Impulsivity and Restlessness

Impulsivity and *restlessness* often go hand in hand in the AuDHD brain. You might speak before thinking, make sudden decisions, or dive into new projects without a clear plan, only to feel overwhelmed afterward. Restlessness can show up as a constant need to move, shift focus, or change your environment just to feel okay. These behaviors aren't careless. They're ways your brain tries to manage discomfort, boredom, or emotional overload. Recognizing these patterns with curiosity, not shame, can help you slow down, check in with yourself, and make choices that support your energy and clarity.

Hyperfocus and Inattention

You may lose track of time when doing something you love. This can feel incredibly productive, creative, and fully alive. But when it ends, you might crash hard, or realize you forgot to eat, sleep, or respond to messages. *Hyperfocus* is not the same as discipline. It's involuntary, and it doesn't always happen when you need it to. On the flip side, *inattention* can make it hard to stay present during tasks that feel boring, repetitive, or overwhelming. You may drift off mid-conversation or reread the same sentence five times. These extremes aren't opposites, they're two sides of the same neurodivergent rhythm, often misunderstood by people who only notice the inconsistency.

Disorganization and Forgetfulness

For many AuDHD women, *disorganization* and *forgetfulness* isn't just about messy desks or lost keys. It's a daily struggle to keep track of time, tasks, objects, and priorities all at once. You might forget appointments, misplace your phone multiple times a day, or start several things without finishing any of them. This isn't because you don't care, it's because your brain is juggling too much without the internal structure that comes more naturally to others. Understanding disorganization as a neurological pattern, not a personal flaw, can help you approach it with more patience and less self-blame.

Retreating Into Fantasy

For some AuDHD women, emotional regulation often comes through *retreating into fantasy*. This could look like daydreaming, escaping into fictional worlds, or mentally replaying ideal scenarios as a way to cope with stress or disconnect from overwhelm. While it can be a creative outlet, it's also a self-soothing strategy, one that may have started in childhood and continued into adulthood as a way to manage emotions when other tools weren't available.

Stimming

Some people also engage in self-soothing behaviors called *stims* or *stimming*: repetitive movements or actions like rocking, tapping, humming, or rubbing textures. These are often unconscious and help regulate the nervous system, especially during stress or overwhelm. Stimming can look different for everyone, and many women do it in subtle ways like hair twirling, skin picking, bouncing a leg, or playing with jewelry.

Executive Dysfunction

This is a big one. *Executive function* is what helps you plan, prioritize, start tasks, finish them, and remember what needs doing. If this part of your brain struggles, it can feel like you're always trying to push through molasses. One expression of executive dysfunction is *task paralysis*, the feeling of being mentally frozen even when you know what needs to be done. You might stare at the sink full of dishes, a deadline, or an unanswered email, completely stuck. Your brain wants to act, but it doesn't know where to begin. This can be especially common when the task feels emotionally loaded or there's no clear first step. Some people also experience *demand avoidance*, where even simple tasks feel overwhelming or triggering just because they're expected or required. *Poor time management* is also common. You may lose track of time or feel like the day slips away without warning. Executive Dysfunction is not a moral failing. It's your nervous system signaling that it needs support, not pressure.

Anxiety and Depression

Many AuDHD women experience chronic *anxiety*, especially in social or performance-based situations. Years of masking, rejection, or being misunderstood can create a constant sense of vigilance or self-doubt. *Depression* often follows, not because something is wrong with you, but because you've spent so long trying to function in ways that don't match how your brain works. These experiences aren't separate from your neurodivergence. They're often the emotional consequences of trying to survive in a world that hasn't supported you.

It's also important to know that all of these traits aren't static. They can shift with hormonal changes, stress levels, life transitions, or even the seasons. You might notice your sensory sensitivity is worse during your menstrual cycle, or that your executive function crashes during periods of high stress. This isn't inconsistency, it's how AuDHD brains respond to internal and external changes.

Why This Combination Is Misunderstood

Because autism and ADHD present differently in women, and even more so when they're combined, many AuDHD women grow up without the right language for what they're experiencing. They might be called sensitive, moody, spacey, smart but unfocused, high-maintenance, forgetful, intense, or dramatic. The words used to describe them don't reflect what's actually happening inside.

Sometimes ADHD traits cover up autism traits. For example, you might come across as outgoing or talkative because of your energy, even if you struggle to connect socially. Other times, autism traits mask ADHD. You might seem calm and focused because you avoid situations that overwhelm you. Teachers, therapists, and even family members may overlook the complexity of what's really going on.

Medical professionals are also trained to think in terms of separate diagnoses. If someone receives an autism diagnosis, they may stop looking further. If they identify ADHD, they may miss the deeper sensory and social processing differences that point to autism. As a result, many women are misdiagnosed, or told they are just anxious or depressed.

It's not uncommon for AuDHD women to spend years trying to manage symptoms that were never correctly named. They build elaborate coping strategies, wear themselves out trying to be "normal," and carry private shame for the things that feel harder than they should.

Therapy can be helpful for people with AuDHD, but finding the right therapist is often a process. It may take time to connect with someone who truly understands neurodivergence, especially in women. But when the fit is right, therapy can help ease overwhelm, untangle old patterns, and build healthier coping strategies. For some, medication can also bring real relief. If you're curious, talking with a trusted doctor or psychiatrist can help you explore what feels right for your body and brain.

Checklist: Do These Traits Sound Like You?

This is not a diagnostic tool, but a way to begin recognizing patterns in your own experience. Check off any that feel familiar:

- [ ] I often feel overwhelmed by noise, lights, smells, or textures

- [ ] I need a lot of quiet time after being social or in busy places

- [ ] I can hyperfocus on things I enjoy, but struggle to start or finish other tasks

- [ ] I am highly sensitive to other people's moods or tone of voice

☐ I sometimes forget basic things like eating, drinking water, or where I put something

☐ I feel emotions very deeply and sometimes unpredictably

☐ I have trouble switching tasks, even if I want to

☐ I have strong preferences and routines that help me feel safe

☐ I often feel like I'm doing everything "wrong" even when others say I seem fine

☐ I have to work harder than others to manage day-to-day life

☐ I've been called sensitive, intense, or scattered most of my life

If many of these feel familiar, you are not imagining it. You're not just being dramatic, forgetful, or disorganized. You're likely responding to the world with a different kind of brain. And now you're beginning to see it for what it is.

∗

Script: How to Explain AuDHD to Someone Who Doesn't Get It

It can be hard to explain AuDHD to someone who only knows the stereotypes. You don't have to tell anyone unless you want to. But if you're ready to talk about it, here's a simple way to begin:

"I recently learned that I have something called AuDHD. It means I'm both autistic and have ADHD. It affects how I process things like sounds, emotions, routines, and attention. A lot of it isn't obvious from the outside, but it's been part of my life for a long time. Getting clarity around it has helped me understand myself better, and I'm learning how to work with my brain instead of fighting it."

You can add more, or say less. You can keep it clinical or personal. The goal is not to convince anyone. It's just to claim the truth of your experience, in your own words and on your own terms.

Chapter 2
The Invisible Girl and Why You Were Missed

Many women live for decades without knowing they are autistic, have ADHD, or both. They go through school, friendships, careers, and relationships sensing that something is off but never quite being able to name it. They learn to manage. They learn to hide. And they learn to blame themselves.

When they finally hear the term AuDHD, something deep inside begins to stir. They recognize themselves in the descriptions. They feel seen by language they had never encountered before. For some, it brings immediate clarity. For others, it brings confusion, grief, or disbelief. How could something so fundamental have gone unnoticed for so long?

The answer has less to do with you, and more to do with what the world has been taught to look for.

What People Think Autism and ADHD Look Like

Most of the early research and public understanding of autism and ADHD has focused on boys. In schools, clinics, and families, the "typical" profile is still often based on external behaviors: interrupting, fidgeting, falling behind academically, or being socially withdrawn in obvious ways. These traits are easier to spot when they are loud, disruptive, or clearly out of step with social norms.

But for many girls, the traits of autism and ADHD show up differently. They may talk a lot, but struggle with true connection. They may seem imaginative or dreamy, but find it hard to focus. They may be excellent students but collapse with exhaustion at home. Instead of being disruptive, they often internalize their distress. Instead of lashing out, they shut down. And because these differences are quieter, they often go unnoticed.

Especially if you were praised for being "a good girl."

The Pressure to Be Good

From an early age, girls are often taught to be agreeable, adaptable, and emotionally aware. You may have heard that you should be helpful, polite, self-controlled, and pleasant to be around. You may have learned that your value came from being accommodating. If someone else needed something, you were expected to respond. If you were upset, you were expected to calm down quickly. If you had a need, you were expected to wait, soften it, or let it go entirely.

These expectations leave little space for neurodivergent traits.

If you were overwhelmed by noise or touch, you may have learned to tolerate it in silence. If you needed routine or struggled with transitions, you may have been seen as rigid or controlling. If you had trouble reading social cues or responding "appropriately," you may have been called awkward or rude. And if you showed strong interest in something specific, you may have been told you were obsessive, dramatic, or intense.

Over time, many AuDHD girls learn to perform what is expected of them. They observe how others act and mimic the behavior. They force eye contact. They rehearse conversations. They pretend to understand jokes they don't find funny. They suppress their discomfort, hide their confusion, and push themselves to match the energy of the people around them.

This is called **masking**, and it becomes a survival strategy. It is a way to stay safe, to belong, and to avoid the shame of standing out. But masking comes at a cost.

What Masking Really Costs

The more skilled you are at masking, the less likely people are to notice you are struggling. They may see someone who is quiet and cooperative. Or someone who is smart and high-achieving. Or someone who is creative and passionate. They see the surface and assume everything underneath is fine.

But masking takes enormous energy. Holding yourself together in public, at work, in school, or even within your family can leave you drained, disoriented, and emotionally raw. Over time, this leads to burnout. And the burnout that comes from long-term masking is not just about fatigue. It is about the slow erosion of your sense of self.

When you spend years acting like someone you are not, it becomes hard to remember who you really are. You may find yourself disconnected from your preferences, unsure of what you enjoy, or unable to tell what you need. You may lose trust in your own instincts. And when you finally drop the mask, even for a moment, you may feel ashamed or afraid. What if people see the "real" you and walk away?

Masking is not a sign that you were never struggling. It is a sign that you were doing everything in your power to keep up. It is a brilliant, exhausting strategy that allowed you to survive in a world that did not recognize you. But it is not meant to last forever.

Why You Were Misunderstood

The traits of autism and ADHD in women often clash with what others expect or want from us. You may have been called sensitive because you noticed things others didn't. You may have been called dramatic because your emotions came quickly and intensely. You may have been called lazy because executive dysfunction made daily life harder than anyone realized. You may have been labeled bossy, moody, or high-strung because your boundaries looked different from other people's.

Many women with AuDHD were never taught to see these traits as signs of a different kind of brain. They were taught to see them as personal flaws.

This misunderstanding often continues into adulthood. You might go to therapy and be treated for anxiety or depression, while the underlying neurodivergence is never explored. You might receive well-meaning advice that only adds to your shame. Try harder. Be more flexible. Think more positively. These suggestions are often given by people who don't understand what it's like to live with a brain that is constantly overstimulated, pulled in different directions, or running on empty.

The truth is that your struggles were always real. You just didn't have the right words for them yet.

When Invisibility Runs Even Deeper

The path to recognition is even harder for women who live at the intersections of multiple forms of marginalization. Women of color, LGBTQ+ women, and those without access to stable housing, healthcare, or supportive school systems are often overlooked entirely. The signs of neurodivergence may still be there, but the chance of being truly seen is much lower. When basic needs are unmet or survival takes priority, there is rarely room to explore the quieter signs of difference, especially when those differences are misunderstood or misread through a biased lens.

Many marginalized women learn early on to adapt quickly, work harder, and avoid drawing attention to themselves. They may have been told they were "difficult," "emotional," or "disrespectful" in ways that reflected prejudice more than truth. A white classmate might be seen as quirky or shy for the same traits that label a different girl as defiant or inattentive. In the medical system, these women are often misdiagnosed, not believed, or never given access to care in the first place. Queer and trans women may feel unsafe sharing their inner world with providers, or worry that their identities will be pathologized instead of honored.

If this was your experience, the journey toward understanding yourself may have taken longer and required more self-trust. You may have had to unlearn not only the idea that something was wrong with you, but also the deeper message that your pain didn't matter. You may still carry anger or grief about the time it took to be heard. That anger is valid. Your story doesn't erase the added layers you've carried, but it does begin to name them. And naming is the first step toward care that actually sees you.

Looking Back With New Eyes

When women begin to suspect they are neurodivergent,

they often look back on their childhood, their friendships, their education, and their work life with new understanding. Memories that once felt confusing now make more sense. The "weird" habits, the overwhelm, the long recovery time after social events, the panic around deadlines. All of it starts to feel more coherent.

That realization can bring relief. But it can also bring grief.

You may grieve for the girl you were. The one who felt out of place but didn't know why. The one who tried so hard to be normal. The one who was punished or ignored when she was actually in distress. You may feel sadness for the ways you learned to shrink yourself, to hide your needs, or to believe you were too much.

You may also feel anger. Anger at the people who dismissed your struggles. Anger at a system that failed to recognize you. Anger at how much harder things were than they needed to be.

These emotions are not wrong. They are part of the healing process. And you don't have to rush through them.

What matters now is that you are beginning to see clearly. You are starting to name things that were once invisible. You are learning to listen to yourself. And slowly, you are learning to trust what you hear.

∗

Journal Prompt
What messages did I absorb about being "a good girl"?

Chapter 3
The Mask You Didn't Know You Were Wearing

One of the most common things women say after learning they are autistic or have ADHD is, "But no one ever noticed." What they often discover later is that they were **masking** the entire time.

Masking means hiding or softening traits that might be judged, questioned, or misunderstood. It's what many of us do to fit in, avoid conflict, or stay safe. For AuDHD women, masking becomes second nature. It doesn't always feel like a conscious choice. It becomes a way of being in the world: a way of moving through school, work, relationships, and daily life without drawing too much attention or creating too much disruption.

Most of us don't know we're doing it until it starts to fall apart.

Masking as Survival

Masking often begins in childhood. You notice that other people seem to connect more easily. They laugh at the right moments, pick up on unspoken rules, and seem to know what to do in social situations without thinking. You may not have felt that same ease, so you started copying what you saw.

You learned how to smile, nod, and respond even when you were confused or overwhelmed. You memorized social scripts, rehearsed conversations ahead of time, or studied facial expressions and body language like a second language. You may have practiced eye contact even when it felt uncomfortable, or forced yourself to stay in noisy, crowded places when your whole body wanted to leave.

This isn't deception. It's adaptation. It's a way to protect yourself in a world that hasn't made space for difference. It's what many neurodivergent women do when they sense that being fully themselves might lead to rejection, criticism, or exclusion.

Masking can help you succeed. It can help you get through job interviews, maintain friendships, and move through situations that feel socially demanding. It can make you appear confident, easygoing, or competent. Even when you're barely holding it together inside.

But masking is not without cost.

What Masking Looks Like

Masking doesn't always look dramatic from the outside. It's often subtle. It can show up as:

- Forcing yourself to make eye contact when it feels unnatural

- Laughing when you don't find something funny

- Mirroring other people's tone, body language, or interests

- Suppressing stims like fidgeting, rocking, or repeating phrases

- Avoiding talking about your interests because they seem "weird" or "too much"

- Withholding your opinions to keep the peace

- Pretending to understand something when you're actually lost

- Pushing yourself through social situations even when your nervous system is overwhelmed

Over time, this leads to a kind of emotional and physical

exhaustion that's hard to describe. You may leave a social event completely depleted. You might crash after work or fall into patterns of shutdown and withdrawal. You may feel disconnected from your own preferences because you've spent so long adjusting to what others expect.

The longer you mask, the harder it becomes to tell where the mask ends and you begin.

When Masking Breaks Down

Eventually, for many women, the effort becomes unsustainable. Sometimes it happens after a major life transition: parenthood, a new job, a move, or a relationship ending. Sometimes it happens slowly, like your energy draining out drop by drop. And sometimes it happens all at once, in the form of **burnout**.

Burnout can look like depression, but it's different. It's often marked by a deep fatigue that no amount of rest seems to help. You may feel emotionally flat, unmotivated, or easily overwhelmed by things that used to feel manageable. You might find yourself withdrawing socially, unable to keep up with conversations, or feeling detached from your surroundings.

Masking can also break down when you start to learn more about yourself. When you finally discover what autism and ADHD actually look like, you might begin to recognize all the ways you've been bending, contorting, and concealing your true self. That awareness can feel freeing, but also destabilizing. You may question who you really are, what you actually enjoy, and what parts of you were just habits designed for survival.

What Unmasking Really Looks Like

Unmasking is often described as a positive thing, and in the long term, it can be. But in the beginning, it's not always easy or graceful.

You might feel more raw, more irritable, or more easily overstimulated. You may discover that you need more rest, more alone time, or more support than you realized. You might struggle with guilt when you start saying no to things you used to force yourself to do. You might grieve the version of you that always pushed through.

Unmasking doesn't mean you stop caring about others or abandon every social expectation. It means you begin to notice when you are hiding yourself, and you start choosing where, when, and how to show up more honestly. It means letting yourself stim when you need to. It means setting boundaries even if others don't like it. It means expressing what you actually feel instead of what you think will make others comfortable.

There is no single way to unmask. It's not a switch you flip. It's a slow unfolding, a process of reconnecting with yourself, and building trust that the real you is worthy of being known.

*

Script: "I'm Learning to Stop Masking"

It can be hard to explain masking to someone who doesn't experience it. You don't have to tell everyone in your life what you're going through, but sometimes a simple explanation helps create space for change.

Here's one way to start:

"I've spent a lot of my life trying to act in ways that felt expected, even when they didn't feel natural to me. I'm learning that I've been masking, meaning I've been hiding or softening traits to fit in or avoid judgment. I didn't even know I was doing it for a long time. Now I'm trying to be more honest about what I need and how I feel. It might look different from what I used to do, but I'm doing it to take better care of myself."

You don't owe anyone a detailed explanation. You can say less or more. You can set the boundary and walk away. You can let people in slowly, at your own pace.

Unmasking is not about proving anything. It's about making room to breathe.

*

Journal Prompt

What parts of myself have I learned to hide in order to be accepted? Which of those might I want to begin reclaiming now?

Chapter 4
Burnout Isn't Just Being Tired

There is tired, and then there is burnout.

Tired can be solved with a nap or a weekend off. Burnout goes deeper. It gets into your bones, your thinking, your sense of who you are. And for women with AuDHD, burnout often becomes a recurring part of life. Not because you are weak or disorganized, but because you have spent years trying to function in a world that was never built with your brain in mind.

Burnout doesn't always come with a warning. It builds slowly. You may not notice it until it becomes impossible to ignore. At first, you might find yourself getting more irritable or distracted. You may start avoiding tasks that used to feel manageable. You might forget things more often, lose your words mid-sentence, or feel like your mind is full of static.

Then, little by little, the weight gets heavier. The exhaustion deepens. And even small responsibilities start to feel impossible.

In some cases, emotional dysregulation can lead to meltdowns or shutdowns: intense, involuntary responses to overwhelm. A meltdown might show up as crying, panic, or emotional outbursts, while a shutdown can look like going quiet, going numb, or completely disconnecting. These responses aren't overreactions. They're signs that your nervous system has reached its limit. Recognizing what leads up to these moments can help you build in earlier support and prevent full overload when possible.

This isn't laziness. It's not a lack of motivation or willpower. Burnout is your nervous system sending a clear message: **I can't keep doing this.**

The Unique Shape of AuDHD Burnout

Burnout in neurodivergent women often includes physical fatigue, emotional exhaustion, and cognitive fog. It can affect every part of your life: how you think, how you feel, how you relate to others, and how you care for yourself.

It can also be hard to explain to people who haven't felt it. On the outside, you may still look like you're functioning. You may still be showing up to work, responding to messages, or managing daily tasks. But inside, it feels like you're running on fumes, holding yourself together by instinct more than intention.

Burnout can also be hard to identify because it shares similarities with **sensory overwhelm** and **depression**. But the causes and the recovery process are different.

If you are experiencing sensory overwhelm, it often comes on quickly. It may happen after being in a noisy room, under fluorescent lights, or during a long day of social interaction. You might feel a surge of panic or irritation, a need to escape or shut down. Once you remove the trigger and give yourself time to decompress, the symptoms usually ease.

Depression, on the other hand, tends to bring a persistent sense of sadness or hopelessness. You may lose interest in things you once enjoyed, struggle with feelings of worthlessness, or experience long stretches of emotional numbness. Depression can affect your appetite, sleep, and overall motivation. Rest alone doesn't resolve it.

Burnout lives somewhere in between. It isn't always sad. It isn't always panicked. Sometimes it just feels like a flatness that spreads through everything. You might still want to do the things you care about, but feel unable to start. You might still believe in your abilities, but feel too worn down to access them. You may be overwhelmed one moment and disconnected the next.

For many AuDHD women, burnout is the result of trying to meet constant demands while managing sensory sensitivity, emotional intensity, executive function challenges, and social expectations, all without adequate support.

Why It's So Easy to Miss

If you've been masking for years, you've likely developed ways to push through discomfort, to stay productive even when you're struggling. You may have learned to ignore the signs that you're nearing your limit. You may even take pride in being the one who gets things done, no matter what it costs you.

This can make it hard to recognize burnout until it becomes severe. You may think, *I just need a day off,* or *I'm just being dramatic.* But deep down, you know it's not that simple. You might feel like you're disappearing inside your own life. Like your body is still going through the motions, but your mind and heart are checked out.

What you're feeling is real. And it has a name.

What Recovery Really Requires

Recovering from burnout isn't about taking a single day to rest and then going back to normal. In fact, going back to "normal" is often what caused the burnout in the first place.

Recovery means reducing the demands placed on your system, not just temporarily, but in a sustainable, lasting way. It means giving yourself permission to do less. To pause more often. To say no when your body says no. And most importantly, it means shifting how you talk to yourself while you heal.

There is often a voice that shows up during burnout. It tells you to hurry up and get over it. It questions whether you're exaggerating. It reminds you that other people seem to manage just fine. This voice is not your fault. It's something you picked up from a culture that values output over well-being.

But you don't have to listen to it anymore.

You can replace that voice with a gentler one. One that says:

- I deserve to rest before I collapse.

- I don't need to prove anything by pushing through.

- Rest is not a reward. It's a requirement.

- My nervous system has limits, and honoring those limits is not selfish.

Recovery may take longer than you expect. Some days, you'll feel more like yourself. Other days, it may feel like you're sliding backward. This is normal. Burnout recovery is not linear. What matters most is that you continue to offer yourself the care and compassion you've so often reserved for others.

Rebuilding Without Shame
As you recover, you may discover that certain parts of

your life no longer fit. You may realize that some routines, relationships, or environments drain you more than they support you. You may feel the need to simplify, to step back, or to make changes that others don't fully understand.

That's okay.

Burnout is often a turning point. It shows you what can no longer be ignored. It calls you to rebuild, not in the image of what others expect, but in alignment with what you truly need.

This rebuilding process can feel slow. You may wonder if you'll ever regain your energy, your creativity, or your sense of joy. But with time, they will return. And when they do, they will come from a place of real capacity, not just survival.

You don't need to go back to who you were before. You get to become someone new. Someone honest, rested, and whole.

*

Journal Prompt

What does my burnout cycle look like? Are there early signs I've learned to overlook? What would it feel like to respond with compassion instead of pressure?

Chapter 5
Making Peace With Your Past

After discovering you're AuDHD, it's natural to start looking backward. Moments from childhood, school, work, and relationships may come flooding in, reframed now with a clarity you didn't have before. You start to notice patterns you missed. You start to ask new questions. And you begin to grieve. Not just the things that happened, but also the understanding you didn't have at the time.

This is one of the most emotionally tender parts of the journey. It is also one of the most transformative.

Looking at your past through the lens of neurodivergence doesn't erase what happened. But it can soften the edges. It can shift the story from *What was wrong with me?* Or *Why didn't anyone see what I needed?* And it can help you offer compassion to the version of yourself who carried so much without ever being given the right name for it.

Reframing Your Childhood

Many AuDHD women were told they were sensitive, difficult, or dramatic as children. Maybe you were picky about food, or disliked certain fabrics, or needed more alone time than other kids. Maybe you were hyperverbal and asked endless questions. Or maybe you were quiet and withdrawn, more comfortable in your own world than on the playground. Either way, your needs likely didn't fit the mold.

If you did well in school, your struggles may have gone unnoticed. Or if you were labeled gifted or creative, people may have assumed you were fine, even when you weren't. Maybe you were overwhelmed by group work, or confused by unspoken social rules. Maybe you melted down at home after holding it together all day. These are signs of a child doing their best to function in an environment that didn't meet them where they were.

It's also possible that your home wasn't a safe or supportive place. Many neurodivergent women grew up in families where their sensitivity was seen as a weakness, or their differences were punished instead of understood. If that was your experience, the grief may run deeper. There may be layers of pain that go beyond being misunderstood, layers that involve being mistreated, dismissed, or even emotionally harmed.

Whatever your childhood looked like, you deserved

support. You deserved to be seen and guided, not shamed and corrected. Understanding that now won't change the past. But it can start to change how you carry it.

Revisiting School and Work

School is often the first place where neurodivergent traits are challenged. You may have struggled to focus in class, to follow instructions that seemed vague, or to keep up with the pace of homework and tests. You might have excelled in one area and floundered in others, with no one stopping to ask why. Group projects, unstructured time, last-minute changes, and social dynamics can be especially hard for AuDHD students. That kind of distress is rarely taken seriously.

Looking back, you might remember feeling confused by things that seemed easy for others. You might remember pushing yourself to succeed, over and over again, until you had nothing left. You may have learned to work ahead so you could cope with your executive dysfunction in secret. Or you may have given up altogether, believing you were lazy or incapable.

The workplace can bring its own version of this. Office politics, unspoken expectations, last-minute changes, loud environments, unclear deadlines: all of it can chip away at your energy. You might have overperformed to avoid being seen as unreliable. You might have stayed silent in meetings even when you had good ideas. You might have quit jobs that drained you or stayed in jobs that felt impossible because you didn't know there was another way.

Now, when you look back, you can see the threads more clearly. You can see the cost of trying to hold it all together. You can understand why you broke down, shut down, or burned out. And you can begin to forgive yourself for not being able to meet expectations that were never designed for your brain in the first place.

Rethinking Relationships

Relationships, either romantic, platonic, or professional, can be a source of both connection and confusion for AuDHD women. You may have felt misunderstood, misread, or unseen in ways you couldn't quite name at the time. You might have been called cold, distant, too intense, or too sensitive. You might have felt like you were always giving too much or too little, never the right amount.

You may have mirrored others in order to fit in. You may have masked discomfort to avoid confrontation. You may have stayed silent when you were overwhelmed or overstimulated, only to explode or shut down later. If you were in relationships where your differences weren't respected, you may have internalized blame or guilt for things that were never fully your responsibility.

Now, you have a new framework. You can begin to ask, *Was I truly difficult, or was I overwhelmed? Was I truly detached, or was I overstimulated and afraid?* You can begin to understand the moments that felt like failures, not as evidence that something was wrong with you, but as signs that you were struggling in a context that never gave you the full picture of who you are.

The Weight of Guilt and the Inner Critic

One of the most painful realizations after a late diagnosis is how much self-blame you've carried.

You may feel guilty for relationships that ended, for opportunities you couldn't hold onto, or for the way you treated yourself when you didn't know any better. You may hear the voice of your inner critic saying you should have tried harder. You should have been more adaptable. You should have figured it out sooner.

That voice is not the truth. That voice is the product of a lifetime spent without the right mirror. It's the result of being measured against standards that were never made for you.

Now, you have the chance to offer yourself something different. Not because everything is fine, but because you can finally see things for what they were. You did the best you could with the information and support you had at the time. That doesn't mean you didn't make mistakes. It just means you get to stop punishing yourself for them.

Grieving What Could Have Been

Alongside the relief of understanding comes grief. You may grieve for the version of yourself who lived so long without answers. You may grieve for friendships that never worked because you didn't know how to express what you needed. You may grieve for the girl who thought she was broken, and for the woman who carried that belief into adulthood.

Grief is not something to rush through. It's not a sign that you're wallowing. It's a sign that you're finally being honest about what this has cost you. And once that grief has space to breathe, something else can begin to grow.

Self-respect. Clarity. Boundaries. Hope.

You are not going back to fix the past. You are going back to make peace with it.

You don't need to rewrite every story. But you do get to tell the truth now. The version of your life where you weren't lazy, difficult, or scattered. The version where you were doing your best with a nervous system that was working overtime to adapt. The version where your struggles were real, your efforts were enormous, and your difference was not a flaw.

Journal Prompt

If I had known I was AuDHD earlier in life, how might things have been different? What parts of me would I have treated more gently?

Chapter 6
Navigating Relationships Differently

Understanding that you are AuDHD doesn't just shift how you see yourself, it often shifts how you see your relationships. As you begin to recognize your needs more clearly, you may find yourself rethinking how you show up with others, what you've tolerated, and what you're no longer willing to carry.

For many women with AuDHD, relationships can feel like a constant balancing act. You may crave closeness but become overwhelmed by too much interaction. You may care deeply but struggle to express it in expected ways. You may try to stay connected while quietly feeling misunderstood, overextended, or emotionally exhausted.

This chapter explores how these patterns show up across different types of relationships: friendships, family, romantic partnerships, and even in the workplace, and how you can begin to approach them with more clarity, boundaries, and care for your own nervous system.

Friendships: When Connection Comes With a Cost

You may have friendships that have lasted years, built on shared history, humor, or loyalty. But as you learn more about your neurodivergence, you might begin to notice how some of those relationships rely on you masking or overextending yourself.

You may have been the friend who always said yes, even when you were depleted. The one who listened deeply but didn't feel heard in return. Or the one who laughed along even when you were confused or overstimulated. You might have told yourself you were just being a good friend, when really you were pushing past your own limits to keep the peace.

Over time, this can lead to **social fatigue**, a slow-burning exhaustion that builds from too many conversations, too many group settings, or too much emotional labor without reciprocity. You may need more time alone than others. You may prefer fewer, deeper connections. These needs are not a flaw in your personality. They are part of how your brain manages energy, attention, and emotion.

As your self-understanding grows, your friendships may shift. Some may deepen with new honesty. Others may fall away, especially if they depended on you always being available, agreeable, or emotionally contained. This can be painful, but it also opens space for relationships that feel mutual, respectful, and safe.

Romantic Relationships: Rejection, Intimacy and Limerence

Romantic relationships can bring both comfort and complexity. If you experience **rejection sensitivity**, you may find yourself second-guessing what your partner thinks, reading between the lines, or becoming flooded with emotion after a small comment or perceived slight.

You might find that you give too much, too quickly. Sharing deeply, bonding fast, and then pulling back when the intensity becomes too much. Or you might struggle to express your needs at all, fearing you'll be misunderstood or too much to handle.

For many AuDHD women, romantic relationships come with unspoken pressure to perform: to be emotionally available, responsive, and affectionate in predictable ways. But if you process feelings differently, or if sensory issues affect your experience of touch, **intimacy** can become confusing or even distressing.

You may also carry guilt for needing more space, quiet, or time to recover after emotional interactions. A supportive partner will understand that your need for solitude is not withdrawal, it's regulation. The more you learn to name your needs clearly, the more your relationships can become spaces of shared understanding, not silent strain.

Another experience some AuDHD women report is **limerence**, a kind of obsessive, idealized infatuation that can feel all-consuming. This isn't simply having a crush. It's a deep mental fixation that may be fed by loneliness, unmet emotional needs, or the dopamine spikes that come with imagining connection. Understanding limerence as a neurodivergent pattern, not a personal flaw, can be the first step toward creating relationships that feel more grounded and mutual.

Family: The First Place You Learned to Adapt

For many neurodivergent women, family was the first place they learned to mask. You may have been raised in an environment where obedience was valued over self-expression, where your sensory needs were dismissed, or where emotional regulation was modeled poorly or not at all.

In some families, the expectation to "just deal with it" runs deep. You may have been praised for being easy-going when you were actually dissociating, or criticized for being dramatic when you were simply overwhelmed. You may have been compared to siblings who seemed more "normal," or asked to accommodate the emotions of others while ignoring your own.

If your cultural background emphasized conformity, self-sacrifice, or emotional restraint, your neurodivergence may have been even harder to recognize. In some cultures, asking for space, naming sensory needs, or expressing distress openly may be seen as selfish or disrespectful. This can leave you carrying years of internalized guilt, even as an adult.

Setting boundaries with family can feel like betrayal. But it is often a necessary step toward healing. You are not required to make yourself available to people who continue to ignore or minimize your needs. You can love your family and still limit your exposure. You can honor your history and still protect your present self.

Workplace Relationships: Performing Competence at a Cost

In professional settings, you may find yourself masking more than anywhere else. You might rehearse conversations before meetings, smile through overwhelm, or mimic what seems socially appropriate. You may feel pressure to keep up with deadlines even when executive dysfunction makes the workflow confusing or unsustainable.

You might be seen as high-performing while silently struggling. Or you may have been labeled disorganized, scattered, or difficult when you were actually trying to navigate unclear instructions or overstimulating environments.

Workplace relationships often include layers of power and formality that make it hard to name your needs. You may worry about being judged, excluded, or seen as incapable. And depending on your job, disclosing your neurodivergence may feel too risky.

While not every workplace is open to change, you can begin by noticing where you're performing and where you feel genuinely supported. You might set quiet boundaries around communication, like turning off notifications or blocking time for transitions between tasks. You might practice asking for what you need in low-stakes moments, slowly building your confidence in self-advocacy.

Building Relationship Safety From the Inside Out

What all of these relationships have in common, whether they are friendships, family ties, romantic partnerships, or workplace dynamics, is that they often required you to hide parts of yourself in order to maintain connection.

Now, you are learning to do something different. You are learning to prioritize safety, not just for others, but for yourself. Emotional safety means you don't have to guess how someone feels. It means you can express discomfort without fear of punishment. It means you are allowed to need rest, to say no, to feel confused, to not be perfect.

This doesn't mean all of your relationships need to be radically changed or cut off. It means you get to approach them with clearer eyes and a more solid sense of self.

*

Script: "I care about you, and I also need time alone to reset."

If you're not used to speaking your needs aloud, it can help to start with something simple. Here's one way to name both care and space in the same breath:

"I care about you, and I really value our relationship. I also need time alone to reset, especially when I'm feeling overwhelmed. It doesn't mean anything is wrong. It just helps me come back more grounded and present. I appreciate your understanding."

This kind of communication is not selfish. It's honest. It builds connection that doesn't rely on performance or guesswork.

*

Journal Prompt

Where in my relationships have I felt safe being fully myself? What patterns am I ready to shift, even if they've been part of my life for a long time?

Chapter 7
Rethinking Work and Self-Worth

For many women, work is more than a job. It becomes tied to identity, self-worth, and belonging. If you've spent most of your life wondering why certain environments drained you, or why you couldn't keep up even when you cared deeply, the discovery of being AuDHD can bring a mix of clarity and grief.

You may look back at your work history and see burnout after burnout, jobs left abruptly, or praise that didn't match how hard you were struggling. You may remember feeling like you were always on the edge of dropping a ball or being "found out". Not because you were unqualified, but because it took so much behind-the-scenes effort to hold everything together.

When your brain processes time, attention, and stimulation

differently, work becomes more than a place of income. It becomes a place of constant adjustment. And when those adjustments go unseen, it becomes a place of silent exhaustion.

The Hidden Cost of Fitting In

In many traditional work settings, success is tied to predictability, social ease, and stamina. There are often unspoken expectations: quick replies, steady energy, small talk, multitasking, last-minute changes, group work, and unclear boundaries between tasks and people.

You may have found ways to manage these things: by staying late to catch up, scripting what you want to say ahead of meetings, or working harder to appear relaxed and in control. You may have earned praise, raises, or promotions. But underneath, you were masking. And masking is exhausting.

Over time, this creates a painful disconnection. You appear capable, even thriving, while inside you're counting down to your next crash. If your energy crashes after a day of meetings, or if you find yourself avoiding even simple emails because your mind is too cluttered to respond, you are not lazy. You are responding to overload.

When these internal struggles are invisible to others, they often go unsupported. And unrewarded.

The Emotional Work of Letting Go

Recognizing that traditional work structures don't serve

you is one thing. Letting go of the idea that you should be able to thrive in them anyway is another.

Many women feel a deep sense of guilt or failure when they realize they can't keep up the way others seem to. You might think, *If I were stronger, I'd manage.* Or, *Other people can do this. Why can't I?*

You're not imagining the difficulty. You are navigating systems that reward a narrow set of working styles and punish difference. Letting go of the belief that you need to conform is not weakness. It is a shift toward self-respect. It may take time. And it may come with grief. The grief of letting go of roles you thought you had to play in order to be okay.

That grief deserves space. It's not a sign you're doing something wrong. It's a sign you're waking up to what has never worked, and beginning to imagine what could.

What Work Can Look Like Instead

Not everyone can quit their job or change careers right away. But understanding your needs gives you more options than you might have realized. Some women find it helpful to restructure how they work. Others explore alternative paths.

Here are a few examples:

- **Remote or hybrid work** that allows you to control your environment, reduce sensory overload, and manage your own pacing

- **Freelance or contract work** that gives you more flexibility to choose when, how, and how much you work

- **Job sharing or part-time roles** that allow you to contribute meaningfully without running on empty

- **Creative or solo-focused work** like writing, design, research, or crafting, where depth and focus are valued more than speed or sociability

- **Project-based work** that allows you to dive deep into one thing at a time rather than juggle multiple inputs at once

- **Supportive teams or neurodiversity-aware workplaces** where clear communication, accommodations, and respect for boundaries are part of the culture

Even within existing jobs, small accommodations can make a big difference: noise-canceling headphones, written instructions, flexible hours, no forced video calls, or permission to decline meetings that aren't essential. These may sound like luxuries, but for a neurodivergent brain, they're often what make sustainable work possible.

A Note on Systemic Change

It's important to name that not all of this should fall on your shoulders. While personal insight and adaptation are powerful, they are not the whole answer. Workplaces need to change too.

Neurodivergent people shouldn't have to burn out to be taken seriously. Employers can create environments that support a broader range of brains by normalizing flexibility, encouraging open dialogue, and valuing rest and focus over performative busyness.

If it feels safe and possible, you can be part of that change. Sharing your needs, asking for accommodations, or helping to advocate for more inclusive policies is not just self-serving. It's paving the way for others like you who have been silently struggling. But it's also okay if you're not ready to advocate outwardly. Taking care of yourself is a form of advocacy too.

What to Ask Yourself About Work

As you think about your current or future work, here are a few questions to guide your reflection:

☐ Does this work support my sensory needs, or constantly push me past them?

☐ Am I able to take breaks without guilt?

☐ Do I feel like I have to perform a version of myself that doesn't match who I am?

☐ Can I speak up when I'm confused, overwhelmed, or need something to change?

☐ Is this work giving me a sense of contribution and alignment or just survival?

☐ Do I feel seen here?

You may not be able to change everything overnight. But noticing these patterns is the first step. From there, you can begin to make small shifts that honor your capacity, protect your nervous system, and rebuild your relationship with work on your own terms.

You are not difficult. You are not broken. You are learning how to work with your brain instead of constantly working against it.

*

Journal Prompt

What kind of work supports my energy, not drains it? What would I choose if I trusted my needs instead of overriding them?

Chapter 8
The Body You May Have Been Ignoring

For many AuDHD women, the body has been a source of confusion, discomfort, or disconnection for as long as you can remember. You may not have known you were missing cues: hunger, thirst, pain, fatigue, until your body suddenly forced you to pay attention. You may have lived most of your life pushing through, only to hit a wall you didn't see coming.

What often gets missed in conversations about neurodivergence is how much the body carries. Not just sensory input, not just energy levels, but history. Many neurodivergent women have experienced **trauma**, whether through chronic invalidation, neglect, abuse, or simply the repeated message that their needs were too much or too strange. That kind of ongoing stress shapes how we relate to our bodies.

You may have learned early on that your body was not safe to trust. That it gave the "wrong" signals, reacted the "wrong" way, or made things harder instead of easier. Over time, you may have learned to ignore it: to override your needs, suppress discomfort, and stay in situations long after your body told you to leave.

This isn't just **interoception**. It's a survival strategy.

When the Body Shuts Its Voice Down

Interoception is your ability to notice internal signals like hunger, thirst, needing the bathroom, pain, temperature, or emotion. For many neurodivergent people, these signals are muted or scrambled. You may not feel hungry until you are dizzy. You may not realize you're in pain until it's acute. You may miss early signs of anxiety until your body tips into panic.

But for those who carry trauma, this disconnection can go even deeper. You might dissociate without realizing it. You might spend entire days in your head, only registering your body once something feels wrong. You might treat your body like a task manager, asking it to function efficiently rather than listening to it as a partner in your experience.

Sleep can be a long-running challenge for many AuDHD adults. Some experience bedtime resistance or racing thoughts at night. Others struggle with staying asleep, waking groggy, or needing more rest than those around them. Sensory sensitivities, anxiety, and difficulty unwinding can all play a role. Addressing sleep isn't just about routine, it's about building a nighttime environment and rhythm that actually feels safe to your nervous system.

Many women come to this realization not through clarity, but through collapse. Mysterious fatigue, illness, or burnout that doesn't respond to the usual solutions. It can be hard to understand what your body is asking for when you've spent decades learning not to listen.

And even if you want to start listening, the world around you may make that difficult.

The World Isn't Built for Your Body

Sensory-unfriendly spaces, long workdays, inaccessible environments, and constant social pressure can all override even the best self-awareness. You may know you need quiet, but be expected to sit through hours of conversation. You may realize your clothes are physically painful, but feel obligated to wear them anyway. You may notice fatigue halfway through the day, but have no space to rest.

When the world doesn't make space for your body's needs, it becomes easier to ignore them. Over time, you may start believing that your discomfort is something to fix privately, not something that deserves accommodation or care.

This isn't just about learning to listen. It's about learning to advocate. And it's about being willing to reimagine how you move through your days. Not to do less, but to live in a way that honors your actual needs.

Medical Gaslighting and Learning to Speak Up

Many AuDHD women have difficult relationships with healthcare. You may have been dismissed, misdiagnosed, or told your symptoms were all in your head. You may have asked for help and left appointments feeling worse than when you arrived. You may have learned to stop asking.

This is common. But it's also deeply harmful. Medical systems often don't understand the connection between neurodivergence and chronic stress, hormonal shifts, pain sensitivity, or fatigue. Instead of listening, they offer quick explanations or mental health referrals that don't address the root cause.

If you've had these experiences, you're not alone, and you're not wrong for feeling wary.

When you're ready, here are a few steps that can help you advocate for better care:

- **Look for providers who specialize in neurodivergent health** or who advertise trauma-informed care

- **Bring written notes** to appointments, including symptoms, questions, and specific concerns

- **Use clear, direct language**, even if it feels unnatural. "I am experiencing [symptom] and I want to understand why" can be more effective than trying to soften your message

- **If possible, bring a support person** or ask for a summary of your visit before you leave

- **If you don't feel heard, you're allowed to seek someone else.** You don't have to stay in the care of someone who invalidates your experience

It can take time to rebuild trust with your own body and with the systems meant to support it. But you deserve care that respects your full experience, not just the parts that are easy to explain.

Returning to the Body, Slowly

You don't have to become perfectly embodied overnight. You don't have to notice every internal signal, feel totally grounded, or commit to a strict wellness routine. The first step is simply to notice: how often do I check in with my body? How often do I override it?

Start small. Begin by asking yourself one or two gentle questions each day:

- Am I hungry? Have I eaten something nourishing today?

- Did I drink enough water?

- How does my body feel in this chair, in this room, in this light?

- Do I feel hot, cold, tense, or spaced out?

- Is my breathing shallow or steady?

- What am I needing right now that I've been ignoring?

These questions are not chores. They are invitations. They are a way to rebuild the relationship between you and the body that has always been trying to care for you, even when you couldn't hear it clearly.

When you pair this kind of awareness with small, supportive choices: rest, food, movement, silence, you begin to make room for regulation. Not as a performance, but as a practice of self-trust.

Daily Regulation Plan (gentle, adaptive checklist)

If you'd like a place to start, this short list can help you shape your day around your body's needs:

- **One thing to remove or reduce:** (noise, sensory irritation, social obligation)

- **One thing to nourish myself:** (warm food, hydration, sunlight, rest)

- **One physical regulation tool:** (movement, stimming, stretching, deep breaths)

- **One moment of quiet check-in:** (a few minutes to feel what's happening internally)

- **One boundary to support my nervous system:** (canceling something, saying no, turning down stimulation)

You don't need to do all of this every day. These are not requirements. They are options. They are small acts of care that help you reconnect. Not just to your body, but to your own inner authority.

*

Journal Prompt

What does safety feel like in my body? How do I know when I am approaching burnout, overwhelm, or shutdown? What helps bring me back?

Chapter 9
Routines That Actually Work for You

If you've struggled with routines your whole life, you're not alone. You may have tried planners, calendars, habit trackers, or productivity hacks. You may have been told you just need more discipline or motivation. You may have believed that if you could only "stick to a routine," everything else would fall into place.

But for many AuDHD women, routines are not just hard to build: they're hard to remember, hard to restart, and hard to adapt when life shifts. This isn't laziness. This is a brain that processes time, memory, and attention differently.

The goal is not to force yourself into a system that doesn't work. The goal is to build a rhythm that supports your energy, respects your nervous system, and gives you something steady to return to, even when things fall apart.

Why Traditional Routines Often Fail

Most routines are built on the assumption that you'll remember each step, move smoothly from task to task, and adjust easily when things change. But if you have **executive function challenges**, these expectations can set you up for constant frustration.

You may forget your routine entirely once the day starts. You may get overwhelmed deciding what to do first. You may remember to do something, but not at the right time. Or you might get stuck between steps, unable to transition.

These aren't moral failings. They're neurological patterns. And once you understand them, you can start designing routines that take your brain into account.

Anchors and Rhythms, Not Schedules

Instead of trying to follow the clock, many AuDHD women do better with **anchored routines**: small, meaningful habits that mark a transition in the day, no matter when they happen.

A **morning anchor** might be something like making a warm drink, opening a window, lighting a candle, or putting on soft clothes. It's not about productivity. It's about signaling to your body that the day is beginning.

Later in the day, a **midpoint reset** can help break the cycle of overstimulation. You might step outside, move your body gently, or sit in silence for five minutes. Even a short pause can help your nervous system shift gears.

At night, an **evening anchor** helps guide your body toward rest. This might include dimming lights, playing calm music, brushing your hair, or simply sitting in the same spot each night to unwind.

The goal isn't to create rigid steps. It's to build consistent *touchpoints*. Moments that help you feel safe, centered, and connected to yourself.

Working With Your Sensory Profile

Another way to shape routines is by understanding which sensory inputs soothe you, and which ones don't.

You might find comfort in gentle fabrics, weighted blankets, dim lighting, soft background sounds, or familiar scents. Or you might find overstimulation creeps in from scratchy clothes, loud spaces, clutter, or bright lights.

Start noticing. When do you feel most grounded? What are your surroundings like? What textures, sounds, and spaces help your nervous system settle? What consistently leaves you feeling overwhelmed?

Your answers to these questions can shape not just your environment, but the *feel* of your daily routines.

Memory Aids and Gentle Reminders

Even flexible routines can fall apart if you don't remember them. That's not a character flaw, it's a memory challenge.

Try using **visual prompts** like sticky notes, a small dry-erase board, or a daily "cue card" that sits near your bed or computer. Keep it simple, five or fewer reminders at a time.

You can also try **habit stacking**: linking a new action to something you already do. For example, if you make coffee every morning, use that time to do a brief body scan. If you brush your teeth before bed, pair that with a few minutes of calming breathwork.

Digital reminders can also help, but they need to work with your attention span, not against it. Consider using alarms with descriptive labels ("Close computer + stretch") or a visual timer with gentle cues.

Whatever you choose, keep it forgiving. If you forget one day, or even many days, it doesn't mean the routine has failed. It just means you need a softer way back in.

When Everything Falls Apart

Even the best routines will break sometimes. You'll have days where you're sick, overstimulated, caring for others, or just not able to follow through. This is normal.

Instead of starting over from scratch, try having a **reset routine**: a very short list of actions that help you feel human again when everything feels too big.

Here are some real-life reset examples:

- After a meltdown: go to a dark room, drink cold water, put on soft clothes, and rest.

- After a workday that drained you: lie on the floor, cover your eyes, listen to instrumental music for ten minutes. No talking.

- After forgetting your plan for the day: reread your cue card, pick *just one* thing to do next, and reward yourself for doing it.

- After a sleepless night: cancel non-essentials, move slowly, eat something warm, speak kindly to yourself. "I'm doing what I can."

The point isn't to get everything back on track. The point is to give your nervous system a bridge back to safety.

Working Within Real-Life Limits

Some women have more control over their days than others. You may have caregiving responsibilities, a full-time job, or environments you can't easily change. You may not be able to step away or adjust your hours. That doesn't mean routine-building is out of reach, it just means you need to work within your real-life scaffolding.

You might try creating **micro-routines**, two- or three-step check-ins that you can fit into transitions you already have, like school drop-offs, commute breaks, or lunch hours. Even sixty seconds of intentional breathing or putting your hand over your heart can shift your system.

You might not be able to control your full schedule, but you can still create *moments* of consistency. Tiny acts of nervous system support that don't rely on a perfect day or a quiet house.

Your routine doesn't need to be impressive. It just needs to be kind.

Daily Regulation Toolkit (in practice)

Here's a gentle structure to build your own toolkit. Use it as a flexible frame, not a checklist to complete.

- **3 sensory inputs I respond well to:** soft blankets, gentle instrumental music, mint tea

- **1 grounding practice I can do in under 5 minutes:** hand on chest, slow breath in and out, noticing five things around me

- **2 things I must remove to feel calm:** loud TV, multitasking, overhead lights

- **1 person or space that feels emotionally safe:** texting my sister, sitting in the parked car, my side of the bed

- **My reset routine for when everything goes sideways:** silence, water, no decisions, one soothing song

Write your own version in a place where you can find it again: your journal, your phone, a note by your bed. You don't have to use it daily. Just know it's there when you need it.

*

Journal Prompt

What helps me feel steady? Not productive, not impressive, just steady? How can I make space for that feeling each day?

Chapter 10
Parenting While Neurodivergent

Parenting is hard for everyone. But when you're neurodivergent, especially when you've only recently discovered it, parenting can feel like trying to hold someone else's world together while your own is still being rebuilt.

Many AuDHD women carry deep love for their children alongside chronic overwhelm. The structure, demands, and emotional labor of parenting often run headfirst into executive dysfunction, sensory sensitivity, and the pressure to stay regulated for someone else's sake. It's a full-body, full-brain experience. One you may not feel prepared for, especially if your own needs were neglected or misunderstood growing up.

And if you're parenting without strong support, a partner who understands, extended family, access to therapy, financial security, the strain can be even greater. You may feel like you're in survival mode more often than not. There may not be time or space to reflect, plan, or reset. You may be doing everything alone, and doing it while masking your own overwhelm. That reality deserves to be acknowledged, without blame.

Still, parenting from this place of self-discovery can also be powerful. You are unlearning in real time. You are breaking cycles, even if it feels messy. You are noticing things you were never allowed to express. That awareness alone is meaningful. It means your child will be seen in ways you were not.

How AuDHD Traits Show Up in Parenting

Many common traits of autism and ADHD can become more pronounced in parenting. You may find it hard to transition between tasks, especially during the morning rush or bedtime routines. You might feel guilt about not being more "present" when your brain is overstimulated or your body is shutting down. You may crave time alone and resent the constant noise, touch, and unpredictability that comes with caregiving, even if you deeply love your child.

You might also struggle with follow-through, executive tasks, or initiating the dozens of invisible steps it takes to maintain a household. Things like remembering forms, packing lunches, managing schedules, or signing permission slips may feel like monumental hurdles. That doesn't mean you're disorganized or incapable. It means your brain isn't set up for the kind of constant micro-tasking that modern parenting often requires.

And yet, your AuDHD brain may also bring powerful gifts to the table, ones that deserve more space and credit.

The Strengths You Bring to Parenting

AuDHD parents are often deeply empathetic, especially to children who express themselves in unconventional ways. You may notice subtle shifts in your child's mood or body language. You may create playful, creative rituals that help your child feel safe and seen. You may have a strong sense of fairness, or a deep respect for your child's autonomy and inner world.

Your pattern recognition may help you anticipate meltdowns before they happen. Your hyperfocus might allow you to dive deeply into your child's interests and join them in their world. Your sensitivity might allow you to co-regulate gently, through tone of voice or body presence, even when words are hard to find.

These are not small things. They're not lesser than productivity or schedule management. They are the foundation of secure connection.

Your parenting doesn't need to look like anyone else's to be good.

Sensory Overload, Executive Dysfunction, and the Invisible Load

Caring for a child means meeting constant needs, many of which come without warning. For AuDHD parents, this can be destabilizing. If you struggle with interoception, time blindness, or auditory sensitivity, you may feel like you're always running behind, snapping too quickly, or retreating to avoid shutdown.

Executive dysfunction makes the invisible load of parenting even heavier. Remembering appointments, managing meals, responding to school emails, helping with homework, and juggling household tasks can feel like an unsolvable puzzle, especially without support.

If you're parenting solo, or while dealing with chronic illness, poverty, housing insecurity, or lack of access to childcare, the pressure is compounded. And for many neurodivergent parents, there is no safety net. Financial stress may show up through reduced work capacity, costly therapies, lack of paid time off, or inaccessible systems.

This isn't a matter of trying harder. It's about needing more support in a system that rarely offers it.

Concrete Tools for Managing Daily Overload

When your brain struggles to hold many tasks at once, externalizing that information becomes essential. Here are a few ways to reduce pressure and simplify routines:

- **Visual schedules**: Post a simple, color-coded chart on the wall for morning and evening routines, both for your child and yourself. Images or icons can help reduce decision fatigue.

- **Task batching**: Set aside one specific time each week for school forms, emails, or meal prep so those tasks don't bleed into every day.

- **Reminders that work for *you***: Use alarms with labels ("switch laundry," "take snack for pickup"), dry erase boards, or sticky notes on high-traffic areas.

- **Pre-set defaults**: Simplify clothing, meals, or school prep by creating go-to defaults. It's okay if your child eats the same few meals. It's okay if you wear the same outfit rotation.

- **Anchor your day**: Choose one "non-negotiable" grounding action (like coffee on the porch, 3 minutes of stretching, or a shower before bed) that supports your nervous system, even on chaotic days.

Small systems reduce decision fatigue. They create more space for presence and reduce the shame spiral of "Why can't I keep up?"

Breaking Cycles of Shame and Overcorrection

Many AuDHD women were raised in environments where their differences were criticized or corrected. You might have been called dramatic, disorganized, defiant, or lazy. You may have been taught to push through exhaustion, to suppress your feelings, or to shrink yourself to make others comfortable.

It's common to carry those internalized messages into parenting. You might hear your own caregiver's voice in your head when your child has a meltdown. You might fear being too lenient or too reactive. You might notice yourself apologizing constantly or overcompensating to prove that you're doing it right.

The work here is not to be perfect, but to be present. To notice when old patterns are playing out, and gently pause. To choose curiosity over control. To admit when you've reacted out of habit, and repair without shame.

You do not have to parent from the same scripts you were given. You can write new ones, even slowly, even imperfectly.

When Your Child Might Also Be Neurodivergent

It's common for AuDHD parents to begin recognizing traits in their children once they've started to see them in themselves. You might notice sensory sensitivities, emotional intensity, trouble with transitions, or a strong need for predictability. You might see a version of your younger self in your child and feel both protective and afraid.

If you suspect your child is neurodivergent, you don't have to rush into a diagnosis. You can start by creating an environment that is flexible, responsive, and safe for their nervous system. You can advocate for them in school, offer language for what they're experiencing, and validate their differences. You can model self-awareness and self-regulation, not because you've mastered it, but because you're learning too.

Whether your child is diagnosed or not, your attunement is one of the most powerful tools you have. Seeing them clearly, without trying to fix, mold, or normalize, is a gift that can rewrite their entire story of self-worth.

*

Scripts and Strategies for Co-Regulation and Repair

You don't need to stay calm at all times. You don't need to react perfectly. What matters most is your ability to come back into connection after disconnection.

Here are some simple, supportive phrases you can try when things get tense or overwhelming:

"I'm feeling really full right now, and I want to take a few deep breaths before we keep talking."

"I love you, even when we're both upset. Let's figure this out

together."

"I didn't handle that the way I wanted to. Can we try again?"

"You're allowed to feel what you're feeling. Let's both take a break and come back when we're ready."

Co-regulation doesn't mean ignoring your own needs. It means grounding yourself enough to be emotionally available and knowing when to step back, ask for help, or repair later.

You can't teach nervous system safety if you never allow yourself to pause. Modeling that pause is powerful.

*

Journal Prompt

What kind of parent do I want to be, realistically and sustainably? What matters most to me in how I show up, even on hard days?

Chapter 11
Advocating for Yourself in a Neurotypical World

Learning you are AuDHD can come with a rush of clarity. Suddenly, things that never made sense start to fall into place. But that clarity doesn't always translate into the world around you. The people and systems you interact with may not share your understanding or language. And that's where advocacy begins.

Advocating for yourself as a neurodivergent adult doesn't always look like a big confrontation. Sometimes it's as quiet as asking for dimmer lights at work. Sometimes it's declining a phone call and following up in writing. Sometimes it's holding the line on your boundaries, even when someone pushes back.

Self-advocacy isn't about getting others to fully understand you. It's about supporting yourself clearly and consistently, even in environments that weren't built with you in mind.

Navigating Medical Appointments, Workplaces, and Systems

It's common for AuDHD individuals to feel uneasy in institutions. Medical offices, HR meetings, school conferences, and government agencies often require quick thinking, assertive communication, and tolerance for sensory discomfort. All things that may be hard when you're overwhelmed or dysregulated.

In medical settings, you may be dismissed, rushed, or misinterpreted. You might forget what you meant to say, minimize your symptoms, or feel ashamed for needing support. In workplaces, you may avoid asking for accommodations out of fear of judgment or retaliation. You may worry that disclosing your diagnosis will change how others see you.

These concerns are valid. The world isn't always safe or welcoming. But you deserve access, clarity, and care. You don't have to share everything to advocate for what you need. And you don't have to do it all at once.

Understanding Your Rights (and Finding Help When You're Overwhelmed)

In many countries, including the United States, adults with documented disabilities such as autism and ADHD, are protected under anti-discrimination laws. These protections often include the right to request **reasonable accommodations** in workplaces, schools, and public institutions. That might mean flexible deadlines, a quiet workspace, written communication, or sensory-friendly environments.

But knowing your rights is only part of the process. For many people, **navigating the system**, especially while burned out or overwhelmed, feels impossible.

You don't have to do it alone. Here are some ways to access help:

- **Disability advocates and legal aid clinics**: Many nonprofits offer free consultations about disability rights, especially for workplace or school issues.

- **Local or national autism and ADHD organizations**: These often have downloadable guides, sample accommodation letters, and helplines for specific questions.

- **Employee Assistance Programs (EAPs)**: If you're employed, check whether your workplace offers EAP support. Some can guide you through requesting accommodations.

- **Online communities**: Neurodivergent forums or support groups often share templates, scripts, and practical advice from lived experience.

You don't need to understand every law to start advocating. Begin with your lived needs. Be specific, be steady, and know that there is help available to walk you through the rest.

Advocating in the Workplace: Realities and Risks

In a perfect world, accommodations would be granted with curiosity and care. But in reality, some workplaces push back. Some employers may dismiss requests, delay indefinitely, or even retaliate, subtly or directly.

If you are concerned about this, consider:

- **Keeping a written record**: Submit requests via email when possible. Follow up on verbal conversations in writing. Keep copies of communication.

- **Framing clearly**: Focus on how the accommodation supports your productivity, not just your preference. Emphasize that it's a tool for you to do your job well.

- **Involving HR or a union rep**: If your manager is resistant, it may help to loop in a neutral third party.

- **Knowing your backup options**: If things escalate, you may have the right to file a formal complaint through the Equal Employment Opportunity Commission (EEOC) or a state-level agency. This is a big step and doesn't need to be your first one, but it's important to know you have legal protections if needed.

If your workplace feels chronically unsafe or inflexible, know that it's not a personal failure to try and find something different. Sometimes the most powerful advocacy is choosing not to stay where you're being diminished.

Building an Advocacy Support System

Self-advocacy doesn't have to be solitary. One of the most helpful things you can do is build a small circle of people who can support you when you're tired, overwhelmed, or unsure. This might include:

- **A friend who can attend appointments with you** and help take notes or speak up when you freeze.

- **A therapist or coach familiar with neurodivergence**, who can help you practice scripts or prepare for conversations.

- **An online support group**, where you can share drafts of messages or roleplay difficult conversations.

- **A workplace ally**, like a trusted coworker who can reinforce your needs behind closed doors.

You don't have to explain everything to everyone. But letting one or two people really see you and support you can change everything.

When asking someone to support you, be direct and specific. Try:

"I'm trying to explain something important to my doctor, and I tend to shut down. Would you be willing to come with me and help if I get stuck?"
or
"I'm sending this email about accommodations. Can I send you a draft to see if it makes sense?"

Letting people in can feel vulnerable. But you don't have to be endlessly self-sufficient to be strong.

Managing the Emotional Labor of Advocacy

Even when it goes well, advocating for yourself takes energy. It can be exhausting to stay clear, to hold boundaries, to explain yourself again and again. You may feel depleted afterward, even if you got what you asked for.

This is normal. Self-advocacy requires mental, emotional, and sometimes physical labor. You're not just speaking up. You're managing tone, suppressing panic, planning contingencies, and staying emotionally steady, all at once.

To protect your energy, try:

- **Scheduling recovery time**: Block off a buffer after difficult appointments or conversations. Even 15 minutes of quiet can help.

- **Using scripts or notes**: Reduce cognitive load by preparing in advance. You don't need to improvise.

- **Letting go of perfection**: Your words don't need to be flawless. Your calm doesn't need to be constant. What matters is your clarity.

- **Debriefing with someone safe**: Talk it out, cry it out, or simply name what felt hard.

You don't have to be endlessly available, endlessly patient, or endlessly composed. You get to take care of yourself, too.

Knowing When to Explain and When Not To

There is no single "right" way to talk about your neurodivergence. Some people find it empowering to be open and name their diagnosis directly. Others choose to focus on specific traits or challenges without using labels. Still others prefer to stay private altogether.

The key question is: *What is the purpose of sharing right now?*

- If you're seeking support, specificity helps.

- If you're setting a boundary, simplicity helps.

- If you're protecting your peace, silence may be best.

You don't owe anyone your full explanation. You get to decide when sharing feels like connection, and when it feels like exposure.

*

Journal Prompt

Where in my life do I want to be more honest about who I am? What would it feel like to ask for what I need, even just a little more than I do now?

Chapter 12
Living As You Are, Not Who You Were Told to Be

For many AuDHD women, life has been shaped by the need to prove something. That you're capable. That you're easy to be around. That you can do what's expected of you, even if it takes everything you have. You may have built a life around being helpful, efficient, productive, or accommodating. Not because it reflected who you are, but because it felt like the only way to belong.

But now that you know what you're working with, how your brain and body actually function, you get to ask a different question.

Who are you, when you're not trying so hard to be someone else?

Reclaiming your identity isn't about making dramatic changes all at once. It's about loosening the grip of other people's expectations so you can begin to hear your own voice again. The quiet one underneath all the coping. The part of you that still knows what it loves, even if it got buried.

You might be someone who needs more rest than others. Someone who likes to repeat certain meals or activities. Someone who feels deeply, notices everything, or drifts off into daydreams. You might stim without realizing it. You might organize your world in ways that look strange to others but make perfect sense to you. You might be quiet around strangers and loud with your people, or the other way around.

Let yourself be that person.

Let yourself be weird, or soft, or intense. Let yourself be analytical, creative, disorganized, methodical, sensitive, or exacting. Let yourself follow routines or resist them. Let yourself love things that don't seem practical. Let yourself stop performing.

The world teaches neurodivergent women that their worth comes from doing, from fitting in, from making others comfortable. But that version of worth is conditional. And it's exhausting.

Your worth doesn't need to be proven. It can simply be remembered.

Building Toward Joy, Not Just Stability

Once you understand your needs and patterns, it becomes easier to build a life that supports them. But support is just the starting point. You're allowed to ask for more than just survival.

What does a joyful day look like? What kind of work, rest, space, or company makes you feel most yourself? What brings you curiosity? What kind of home makes your body relax? What kind of interactions leave you feeling safe and seen?

These aren't luxury questions. They are central to designing a life that actually fits.

You don't need a perfectly balanced schedule or a flawless morning routine. You need space for your natural rhythms. You need enough clarity to make choices that feel right to you. You need a little room to follow what feels good, even if you can't explain why.

A good life isn't one that looks like everyone else's. It's one that makes sense in your own nervous system.

*

Journal Prompt

What does a good life look like for me now? Not in theory, not for someone else, but in my actual body and mind?

Conclusion
You Were Always Enough

You weren't broken. You weren't lazy or too much or not enough. You were just wired differently.

All those years you spent trying to fit in, to work harder, to make sense of things that felt confusing or overwhelming, you were doing the best you could without the full picture. And now that you have that picture, the past may feel different. Sharper, clearer. Sometimes heavier. Sometimes lighter.

A late diagnosis doesn't undo the pain of being misunderstood. It doesn't give back the time spent masking or the energy lost in trying to meet impossible expectations. But it does offer something real: a new beginning. A language for what you've lived. A mirror that finally reflects you accurately. And permission to stop pretending.

This isn't about becoming someone new. It's about becoming more fully yourself. The parts of you that were hidden, quieted, or shamed didn't disappear. They waited.

They endured. And now, they get to come forward.

You get to unlearn the rules that never fit. You get to create a rhythm that supports your body and mind. You get to ask for what you need, even if your voice shakes. You get to rest, to stim, to change your mind. You get to live in a way that feels safe, sustainable, and real.

This book isn't the end of your journey. It's the beginning of a deeper one. One built not on fixing yourself, but on understanding yourself. Not on striving for acceptance, but on rooting into self-trust. Not on proving your worth, but on knowing it.

You've already survived so much. Navigating a world that didn't see you clearly. And still, you adapted. You stretched. You showed up. Now it's time to live in a way that honors who you are, not just what you can endure.

You were always enough. You always will be.

And now, you finally get to live like it.

About the Author

Sarah Jones is a writer and advocate who focuses on the lives of women with AuDHD. She writes to help others feel seen, understood, and supported, especially those who were diagnosed later in life. She lives in the Pacific Northwest with her rescue dog, a bookshelf that's always overflowing, and a deep love for quiet mornings.

www.ingramcontent.com/pod-product-compliance
Lightning Source LLC
Chambersburg PA
CBHW061746050726
47598CB00002B/602